Saint-Jean-Baptiste Day

Jessica Morrison

Weigl

Published by Weigl Educational Publishers Limited
6325 10th Street S.E.
Calgary, Alberta
T2H 2Z9

www.weigl.com
Copyright ©2011 WEIGL EDUCATIONAL PUBLISHERS LIMITED

Library and Archives Canada Cataloguing in Publication data available upon request.
Fax 403-233-7769 for the attention of the Publishing Records department.

ISBN: 978-1-55388-616-7 (hard cover)
ISBN: 978-1-55388-617-4 (soft cover)

Printed in the United States of America in North Mankato, Minnesota
1 2 3 4 5 6 7 8 9 0 14 13 12 11 10

062010
WEP230610

Editor: Josh Skapin
Design: Terry Paulhus

Weigl acknowledges Getty Images as its primary image supplier for this title.
Alamy: pages 5, 9, 13, 21.

We gratefully acknowledge the financial support of the Government of Canada through the Canada Book Fund for our
publishing activities.

Contents

What is Saint-Jean-Baptiste Day?

French Canadian culture and heritage are honoured on Saint-Jean-Baptiste Day. This holiday is celebrated in the province of Quebec and by Francophones across Canada. It is held on June 24 each year.

4

Saint John the Baptist

Saint-Jean-Baptiste Day is named after Saint John the Baptist. Saint John the Baptist was the Jewish preacher who **baptized** Jesus Christ. In 1908, Saint John the Baptist was declared the patron saint of French Canadians. This means that he is a symbol of all French Canadians.

Canada's First Celebrations

One of the first Saint-Jean-Baptiste Day celebrations in Canada was in the 1630s. Fur trappers and traders sang and ate together along the St. Lawrence River. They also lit bonfires.

Lighting Bonfires

Bonfires are a tradition on Saint-Jean-Baptiste Day. This tradition started thousands of years ago. The king of France lit a bonfire each year in honour of Saint John the Baptist. French colonists from Europe brought this tradition with them to Canada.

11

French Canadians Unite

Ludger Duvernay was a newspaper **editor**. He wanted French Canadians to celebrate their culture. On Saint-Jean-Baptiste Day in 1834, Duvernay hosted a feast for French Canadians. He also created the Saint-Jean-Baptiste Society. This group promotes French culture in North America.

Quebec Holiday

Quebec City held its first official Saint-Jean-Baptiste Day in 1842. In 1925, Saint-Jean-Baptiste Day became a holiday in the province of Quebec. It became known as the national holiday of Quebec in 1977. The holiday is also called "la Saint-Jean" and "Fête nationale du Québec."

14

Special Celebrations

Many people in Quebec do not have to work or go to school on Saint-Jean-Baptiste Day. Sometimes, people celebrate by holding large outdoor events. These events may include rock or jazz **concerts** and fireworks displays. Sports tournaments are also held on Saint-Jean-Baptiste Day.

Family Time

Some people celebrate Saint-Jean-Baptiste Day with their family. They may take part in small neighbourhood events, such as **yard sales**, picnics, or barbecues. Some families attend church on Saint-Jean-Baptiste Day.

Fleurs-de-lis

The fleurs-de-lis is a drawing of a lily. It is a symbol of Saint-Jean-Baptiste Day and Quebec. The word *fleur* means "flower." *Lis* means "lily." Some people paint a fleur-de-lis on their face on Saint-Jean-Baptiste Day.

French Canadian Colours

French Canadians often wear blue and white clothing on Saint-Jean-Baptiste Day. These colours are symbols of Quebec. They are used on the province's flag.

22

23

Glossary

baptized	concerts
editor	yard sales

Index